CATERPILLARS

FIND • IDENTIFY • RAISE YOUR OWN

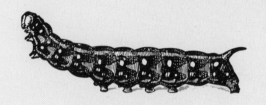

Chris Earley
with Skye Earley

FIREFLY BOOKS

A Firefly Book

Published by Firefly Books Ltd. 2013

The publisher gratefully acknowledges the financial support for our publishing program by the Government of Canada through the Canada Book Fund as administered by the Department of Canadian Heritage

First printing

Publisher Cataloging-in-Publication Data (U.S.)

Earley, Chris.
    Caterpillars : find, identify, raise your own / Chris Earley
[32] p. : col. photos. ; cm.
Summary: Tips and tricks on how to find, identify, feed and care for caterpillars, butterflies and moths.
ISBN-13: 978-1-77085-182-5
ISBN-13: 978-1-77085-183-2 (pbk.)
1. Caterpillars—Juvenile literature. 2. Butterflies—Juvenile literature.
3. Moths—Juvenile literature. I. Title.
595.78139 dc23   QL544.2.E374 2013

Library and Archives Canada Cataloguing in Publication

Earley, Chris G., 1968-
    Caterpillars : find, identify, raise your own / Chris Earley.
Includes bibliographical references.
ISBN-13: 978-1-77085-182-5 (bound).
ISBN-13: 978-1-77085-183-2 (pbk.)
1. Caterpillars--Juvenile literature. 2. Caterpillars as pets--Juvenile literature. 3. Caterpillars--Identification--Juvenile literature. I. Title.
SF459.C38E27 2013   j638'.5781392   C2012-906721-0

Published in the United States by
Firefly Books (U.S.) Inc.
P.O. Box 1338, Ellicott Station
Buffalo, New York 14205

Published in Canada by
Firefly Books Ltd.
50 Staples Avenue, Unit 1
Richmond Hill, Ontario L4B 0A7

Cover design: Erin R. Holmes/Soplari Design

Printed in China

Dedication

To Jiffy/Mummy,
Thanks for putting up with a kitchen full of caterpillars every summer!
Love Chris and Skye

Acknowledgments:

Special thanks to our friends, neighbors, University of Guelph Arboretum staff and Guelph Lake Interpretive Centre staff for bringing us caterpillars. This book wouldn't have been possible without the additional photos provided by Stephen Marshall, Candice Talbot, Jason Dombroskie, Nolie Schneider, Kyle Horner and Henry Kock. Thank you! Thanks also to Christen Thomas and Michael Worek, our fine editors and Erin Holmes for her wonderful book design.

Photo Credits

All photos are © Chris Earley with the following exceptions. Page 5: (caterpillar illustration) ©Shutterstock.com/3drendering; page 6: (adult laying eggs) © Henry Kock, (close-up of eggs) © Shutterstock.com/AlessandroZocc; page 9: (monarchs mating) © Shutterstock.com/Keren; page 13: (caterpillar in jar) © Carrie Cook; page 17 (Io adult caterpillar) © Stephen Marshall; page 21: (Red-Spotted Purple caterpillar) © Kyle Horner; page 22: (Cabbage White adult) © Shutterstock.com/Mirvav; page 23: (Wild Cherry Sphinx adult) © Nolie Schneider, (Abbot's Sphinx caterpillar) © Stephen Marshall, (Abbot's Sphinx adult) © Candice Talbot, (Paddle caterpillar adult) © Jason Dombroskie; page 25 (Lace-capped Prominent adult) © Candice Talbot; page 26 (Red-fringed Emerald adult) © Candice Talbot, (Camouflaged Looper adult) © Jason Dombroskie; page 27 (Filament Bearer adult) © Stephen Marshall; page 28 (Eight-spotted Forest caterpillar and all adult images) © Stephen Marshall; page 29 (Forest Tent and White-marked Tussock adults) © Stephen Marshall; page 30: (Spotted Tussock adult and Virginia Ctenucha adult) © Stephen Marshall, (Milkweed Tussock adult) © Candice Talbot; page 31 (all adult images) © Stephen Marshall.

contents

What Is A Caterpillar?

A caterpillar looks like a worm with legs, but it is actually an insect. It will change or metamorphose into a moth or butterfly. So a caterpillar is really a baby butterfly or baby moth.

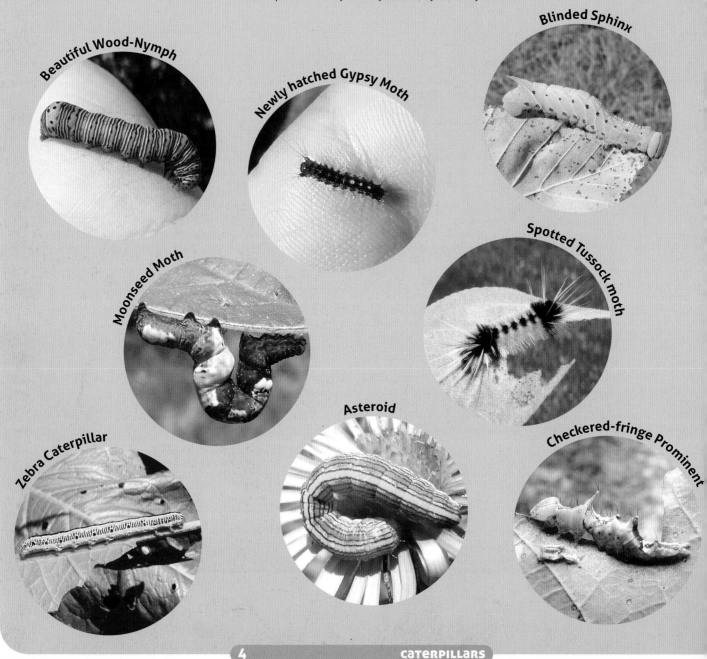

Beautiful Wood-Nymph

Newly hatched Gypsy Moth

Blinded Sphinx

Moonseed Moth

Spotted Tussock moth

Asteroid

Zebra Caterpillar

Checkered-fringe Prominent

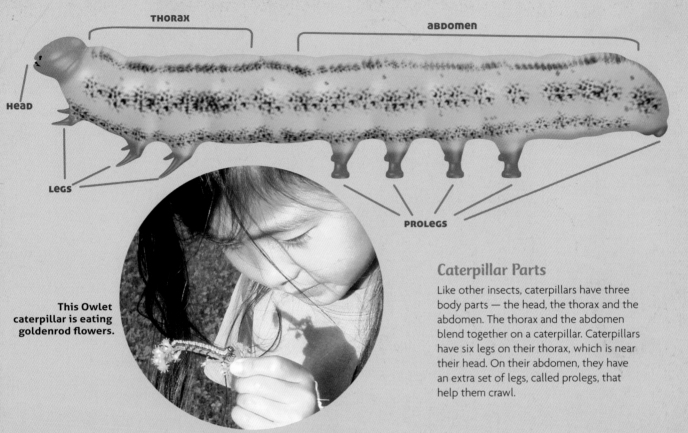

THORAX

ABDOMEN

HEAD

LEGS

PROLEGS

This Owlet caterpillar is eating goldenrod flowers.

Caterpillar Parts

Like other insects, caterpillars have three body parts — the head, the thorax and the abdomen. The thorax and the abdomen blend together on a caterpillar. Caterpillars have six legs on their thorax, which is near their head. On their abdomen, they have an extra set of legs, called prolegs, that help them crawl.

Watching Caterpillars

There are lots of interesting things to see when watching caterpillars.

Some of them tickle when they crawl on your skin.

You can't really see their mouths open and close very well because their jaws are underneath their giant heads. But you can watch them eat leaves because the leaves slowly disappear.

If you put one on a stick, its very back prolegs move first, then the next prolegs, then the next prolegs all the way to its real legs. It is a very smooth motion.

This Polyphemus Moth caterpillar is moving smoothly along a thin stick.

Life Cycle

There are four stages to a butterfly or moth's life cycle, the egg, caterpillar, chrysalis or cocoon and adult stages. How long it takes from start to finish depends on the kind of butterfly or moth.

Egg Stage

A female butterfly or moth usually lays her eggs near or on a leaf that the baby caterpillars will eat after they hatch out of the eggs.

This Mourning Cloak butterfly is laying eggs on a tree. The baby caterpillars will eat the leaves.

Caterpillar Stage

Caterpillars are tiny when they come out of their eggs. But they are going to eat a lot and grow quickly. When they get too big for their skin they just crawl out of it wearing the new, roomier layer of skin that had grown underneath. This is called molting. Some caterpillars even eat their old skin!

You can't take care of some caterpillars during the winter because they hibernate under the snow. Wooly Bear and Yellow Bear caterpillars hibernate as a caterpillar, but not in their cocoon or as adults.

This Wooly Bear caterpillar spent the winter under some dead leaves in our garden.

This Yellow Bear is eating her old skin! She was yellow before but is now orange.

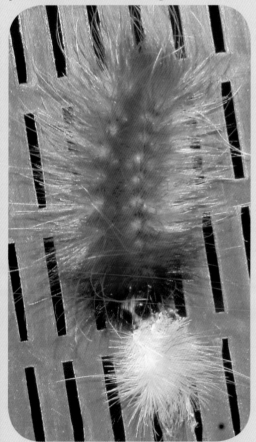

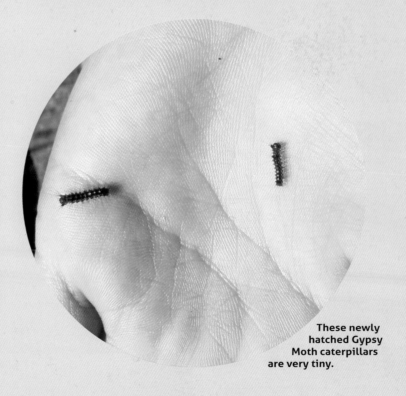

These newly hatched Gypsy Moth caterpillars are very tiny.

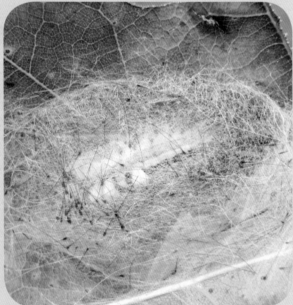

Chrysalis or Cocoon Stage

Caterpillars that turn into butterflies make chrysalises, and caterpillars that turn into moths make cocoons. Some kinds emerge during the summer, and other kinds stay in their chrysalis or cocoon all winter long and then emerge in the spring. Some caterpillars make their cocoons underground, so you may need to put dirt in your container with them. Overwintering cocoons and chrysalises (also called pupae) should be kept outside in a garage or shed, or they might emerge too early.

This Giant Swallowtail caterpillar is getting ready to make her chrysalis.

This White-marked Tussock Moth caterpillar is making a cocoon using some of his own hairs.

This is what the chrysalis looked like when she was done.

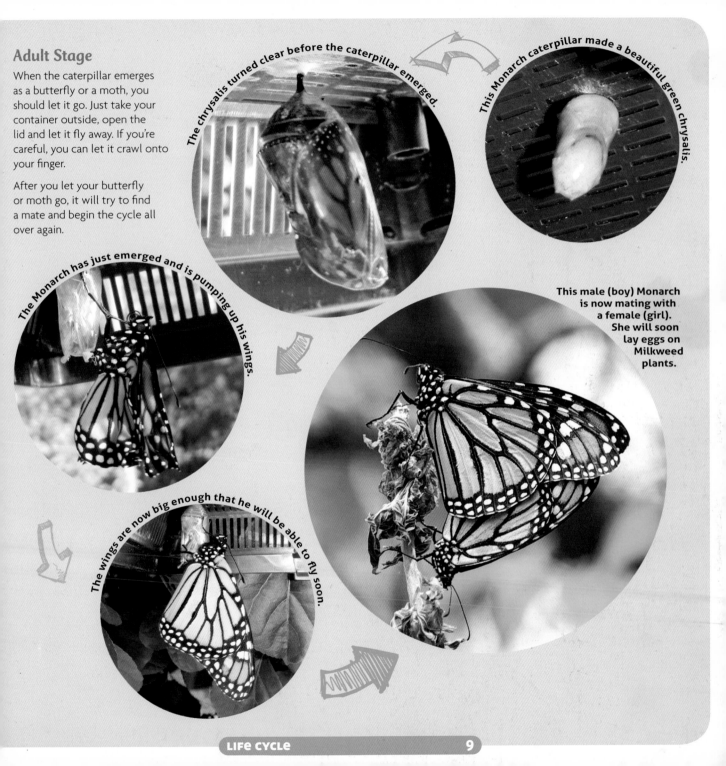

Adult Stage

When the caterpillar emerges as a butterfly or a moth, you should let it go. Just take your container outside, open the lid and let it fly away. If you're careful, you can let it crawl onto your finger.

After you let your butterfly or moth go, it will try to find a mate and begin the cycle all over again.

The chrysalis turned clear before the caterpillar emerged.

This Monarch caterpillar made a beautiful green chrysalis.

The Monarch has just emerged and is pumping up his wings.

The wings are now big enough that he will be able to fly soon.

This male (boy) Monarch is now mating with a female (girl). She will soon lay eggs on Milkweed plants.

Polyphemus Moth Life Cycle

1

These Polyphemus Moth eggs are shown next to my thumb to indicate how small they are.

The caterpillar just hatched out of her egg.

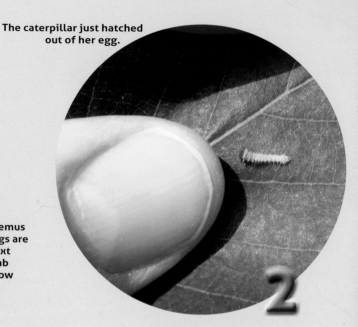

2

5

She has just emerged from her cocoon and is pumping up her wings.

Her wings are almost formed.

6

3

This is the same caterpillar when fully grown.

The caterpillar is in her cocoon.

4

7

Now her wings are done and drying.

The adult moth spreading out her wings and ready to fly.

8

A Caterpillar of Your Own

Although a caterpillar isn't a pet in the same way that a dog or a cat might be, it can still be really fun to find them and to care for them. You can even name one Spot!

How to Find and Hold a Caterpillar

Caterpillars are found in trees or bushes or on the ground. Look for leaves with chewed edges; you may find a caterpillar nearby. Look slowly and carefully and have a container that you can put it in.

If you see a caterpillar, don't grab it with your fingers. Some are very delicate and you could hurt them. Put your hand near the caterpillar, and let it crawl on your hand and then put it in your container.

Be aware! Sometimes caterpillars might poop on your hand because they eat a lot. If they do, don't be alarmed. Just put the caterpillar down and wash your hands with soap and water.

This Yellow Bear just pooped on my finger!

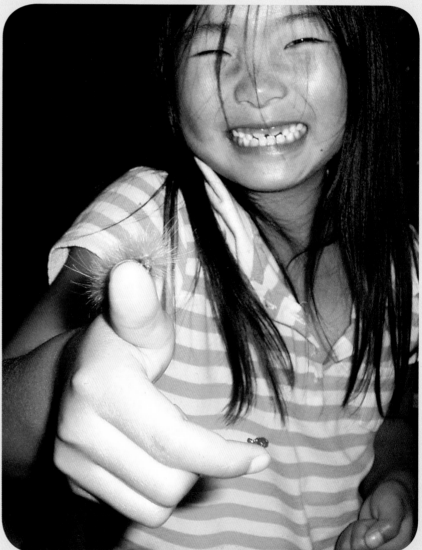

What to Put Your Caterpillar In

You can put your caterpillar in a large jar. Plastic jars are better than glass jars because they won't break. Make sure you put holes in the lid to let in air. You can also go to the pet store or dollar store and get a plastic container for your caterpillar.

You should put a stick in the container so the caterpillar can make a chrysalis or a cocoon that can hang down. Find out how big the adult moth or butterfly will be because the container needs to be big enough for it to spread its wings when it hatches out.

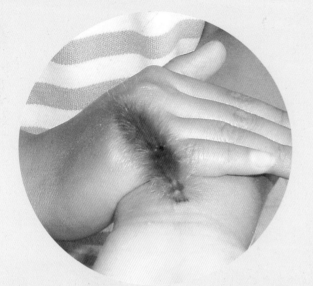

How to Care for Your Caterpillar

Clean out its jar every day or two. Take the caterpillar and old leaves out and rinse the jar with water. Be sure to dry the jar carefully so it doesn't go moldy inside. Then put your caterpillar and its fresh new leaves back in. Wash your hands when you are done.

How to Feed Your Caterpillar

When you feed your caterpillar, make sure you get the right type of leaves. If your caterpillar was eating leaves when you found it, get more of those leaves. Feed your caterpillar once a day. Throw away the old leaves.

This Milkweed Tussock Moth caterpillar only eats milkweed.

This Spotted Tussock Moth caterpillar is eating an apple leaf. They can eat a lot of different tree leaves, such as maple, alder, willow, cherry, oak, basswood and poplar.

When Things Go Wrong

Sometimes caterpillars die because of little bugs in their bodies. These bugs are called parasitoids. Although it's sad if your caterpillar dies, the parasitoids are important because they help keep caterpillar numbers down. If there are too many caterpillars, they could eat too many leaves and kill trees and damage forests.

Some of the parasitoids are flies and some are little non-stinging wasps. Sometimes the parasitoids get into the cocoon with the caterpillar and eat it in there.

This Sphinx caterpillar has a lot of wasp cocoons attached to it.

These fly cocoons came out of some Eastern Tent caterpillar cocoons.

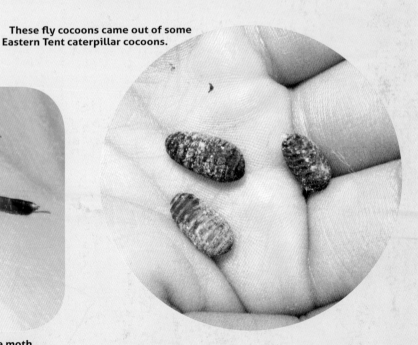

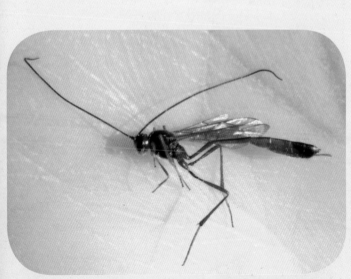

This wasp hatched out of a moth cocoon instead of the moth.

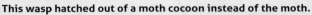

How You Can Help Caterpillars

Teach others about caterpillars! Teach your friends, your family, your teacher, your neighbors and anyone else who wants to know about caterpillars.

You can also help caterpillars by planting flowers that attract butterflies, moths and other insects like bees into your garden. Include plants with leaves that caterpillars like to eat (see the How to Identify Caterpillars section on page 18 for more information about this.)

My dad, my brother and me with my Giant Swallowtail and her mate.

I planted dill in my garden so it could be food for Black Swallowtail caterpillars.

Rules for Raising Caterpillars

This Paddle Caterpillar didn't eat for two days so I let him go.

1. You need an adult to help you. They can remind you to feed your caterpillar and make sure you give it the right food.

2. If you are a beginner, only keep one caterpillar at a time.

3. If your caterpillar isn't eating after two days you should let it go.

Laws About Caterpillars

You can't take anything living home with you from a national, state or provincial park or conservation area. Some caterpillars are endangered, which means there are not too many of them. You should leave them alone so they can make more of their species in the wild. Find out about the laws about caterpillars, butterflies and moths in the place you live.

I found this Smartweed Caterpillar in a park. It looks a bit like a clown with a lot of colorful make-up. My dad took a photo, and we left the caterpillar in the park.

The Io Moth caterpillar has stinging spikes so you shouldn't pick it up!

The Spiny Oak Slug caterpillar's spines can hurt, too. It is colorful to warn predators that it stings and should be left alone.

Dangerous Caterpillars

Caterpillars with hairs or spikes might be able sting you. Don't pick one up with your bare hands if you aren't sure what kind it is. Get to know which caterpillars in your area have poisonous hairs or spikes.

Some people are even allergic to the hairs on fuzzy caterpillars like Wooly Bears, Tussock Moths and Gypsy Moths, so be careful when you first pick them up.

How To Identify Caterpillars

Caterpillars come in many different colors and shapes. Some are fat and some are skinny. Some are big and some are small. Some are fuzzy and some are smooth. Some only eat a certain type of leaf and some will eat almost anything! Shape, size and color will help you identify your caterpillar so you can give it the right food.

There are several books that can help you identify your caterpillar and tell you what to feed it. They are listed on the last page of this book. You can also look on the Internet. Try bugguide.net or www.butterfliesandmoths.org.

The pictures on the following pages show some of the most common and distinctive caterpillars. You can use them to identify some of the caterpillars you will find and learn what they eat. There are also photos of the adult butterfly or moth to show what the caterpillar will become.

This is a Question Mark caterpillar, and it eats hackberry, elm, nettles and hops.

Cecropia Moth caterpillars are very fat and look as if they have different-colored ladybugs stuck to them.

This fuzzy caterpillar is called a Banded Tussock Moth.

Giant Swallowtail

To help it hide from predators, this caterpillar looks like a piece of bird poop! The horns on its head come out when it is touched and are used to try to scare away predators.

Food Plants: hop-tree, prickly-ash and orange leaves

Tiger Swallowtail

Tiger Swallowtail caterpillars can be green or brown. They have spots that look like big eyes; this may make them appear like small snakes instead of tasty caterpillars. They may even move their heads back and forth to scare predators away.

Food Plants: Many tree leaves including cherry, ash and tulip-tree

Black Swallowtail

This caterpillar can often be found in herb gardens. It is sometimes called the Parsley Worm.

Food Plants: dill, parsley, carrots, Queen Anne's lace

Mourning Cloak

Mourning Cloak caterpillars have spikes so that predators don't eat them. The adults spend the winter under tree bark and then emerge in the early spring.

Food Plants: elm, birch willow and poplar leaves.

American Lady

The American Lady has dots and spikes and is quite beautiful. The caterpillar uses its silk to tie leaves together to make a shelter it can use while it eats.

Food Plants: small plants such as pussy toes and pearly everlasting.

Painted Lady

This caterpillar makes a nest by folding a leaf together with silk. The bottom of the nest often fills up with poop.

Food Plants: thistle, hollyhock, burdock

Question Mark

The Question Mark butterfly gets its name from a silver question mark shape on the adult's wing. The chrysalis has beautiful gold spots.

Food Plants: hop vine, elm, hackberry and nettle.

Eastern Comma

It looks like the spines on this caterpillar might sting, but they don't. The adult has a silver comma shape on its hind wing.

Food Plants: nettle, hops, elm

Red-spotted Purple

This caterpillar pretends to look like bird poop, just like the Giant Swallowtail. It looks very similar to Viceroy and White Admiral caterpillars; they are relatives.

Food Plants: oak, cherry and poplar

Monarch

Both ends of the Monarch look the same, so it is hard to tell which end is the head. They eat milkweed leaves and are poisonous to animals that might like to eat them. Their brightly striped bodies warn predators to stay away.

Food Plant: milkweed

Cabbage White

Gardeners might have to compete with these caterpillars for their cabbages. This caterpillar was accidentally introduced to North America from Europe.

Food Plants: cabbage, broccoli

Silver-spotted Skipper

Some caterpillar predators and parasitoids find their prey by smelling for caterpillar poop. Silver-spotted Skippers stop this from being a problem by flinging their poop up to 5 feet (1.5 meters) away from their home!

Food Plants: false indigo, wisteria and locust.

Wild Cherry Sphinx

This large caterpillar has a pretty pink horn and stripes. Like many other sphinx moth caterpillars, it turns into a pupa underground.

Food Plants: cherry, apple

Abbott's Sphinx

Instead of a horn on the end of its abdomen like other sphinx caterpillars, this one has a fake eye that may scare predators away. Some Abbott's Sphinx caterpillars are all brown and others have beautiful green blotches.

Food Plants: grape, Virginia creeper

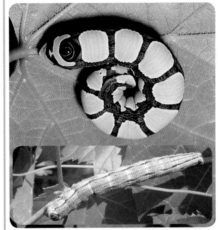

Paddle Caterpillar

This caterpillar makes its cocoon in wood. This caterpillar isn't found very often which is too bad because it looks cool!

Food Plants: many trees, such as birch, poplar, elm and oak

Cecropia Moth

The Cecropia is the biggest caterpillar found in Canada and the United States! It can grow to 4 inches (10 centimeters) long and be very fat.

Food Plants: many different tree leaves such as lilac, apple, ash and cherry.

Luna Moth

This is another big, fat, green caterpillar. The adult is green, too, and has long tails and a fuzzy white body. We find the caterpillars crossing roads in late summer, when they are out looking for a place to make their cocoons.

Food Plants: many different tree leaves such as birch, hickory and walnut.

Polyphemus Moth

This caterpillar is very pudgy. It can make a clicking sound with its jaws that can be quite loud, but no one knows why it does this.

Food Plants: many different tree leaves such as birch, elm, maple, oak and willow.

Rosy Maple Moth

The young caterpillars are found in groups but as they get older they move off to find their own leaves.

Food Plants: maple and sometimes oak

Lace-capped Prominent

This caterpillar hides from predators by looking like a dying edge of a leaf.

Food Plants: beech, oak and birch

Black-blotched Schizura

This species is good at camouflage for its whole life cycle. As a caterpillar, it looks like the dying edge of a leaf. As an adult, it looks like a curled up dead leaf or broken twig. Sneaky!

Food Plants: many different tree leaves but likes walnut and hickory the best.

Red-fringed Emerald

This caterpillar is shaped like oak catkins (the male oak flowers) so it stays hidden. There are other species of emeralds that look like this caterpillar, too.

Food Plants: oak, birch, walnut and others

Camouflaged Looper

This caterpillar covers itself with flower petals so it can hide. This individual was eating goldenrod and so that is why it is decorated with yellow petals.

Food Plants: goldenrod, aster, yarrow, daisy and other plants

Elm Spanworm

The Elm Spanworm is so thin it looks like a stick, which helps it hide from predators. It is an inchworm caterpillar and moves its back up and down as it crawls forward.

Food Plants: elm as well as other trees leaves such as maple, oak, beech and basswood.

Filament Bearer

The Filament Bearer is named after the long filaments on its abdomen. The caterpillar can make them longer when it feels threatened.

Food Plants: many different plants including ash, hemlock, maples, willow, spruce and even strawberry leaves.

Toadflax Brocade

The Toadflax Brocade caterpillar was brought to North America from Europe to eat toadflax which is considered a weed in many areas. It may use its own poop as part of its cocoon!

Food Plant: toadflax

Brown-hooded Owlet

This colorful caterpillar eats flowers instead of leaves. We named the one we raised Rainbow.

Food Plants: goldenrod and aster flowers

Eight-spotted Forester

When you pick up this caterpillar, you might be in for a surprise; sometimes they will barf an orange liquid onto you!

Food Plants: grape, Virginia creeper

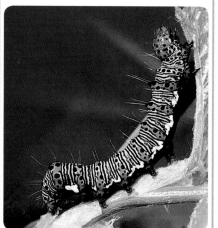

Gypsy Moth

When they are very young, these caterpillars can travel by "ballooning." To do this, they let out a strand of silk until it catches in the wind and then they float off!

Food Plants: over 500 species of plants but they really like hickory, oak and beech.

American Dagger

The American Dagger caterpillar looks like it's wearing a giant wig. They can be white or yellow with big black tufts.

Food Plants: many different tree leaves, such as maple, oak, birch, elm, poplar and hickory.

Eastern Tent Caterpillar

This caterpillar is well known for the silk tents that it makes on trees. The caterpillars live in the tent but go outside to eat.

Food Plants: many different tree leaves but young caterpillars like cherry and apple the most.

Forest Tent Caterpillar

Interestingly, the Forest Tent caterpillar doesn't make a tent! But it does live in groups. You can tell this caterpillar from the Eastern Tent caterpillar because it has small penguin shapes on its back.

Food Plants: many different tree leaves such as maple, oak, poplar and birch.

White-marked Tussock Moth

This is the punk rocker of the caterpillar world. Nice hairdo! The adult female of this species can't fly, but, like other female moths, she can still attract mates with her smell.

Food Plants: many different tree leaves such as oak, apple, cherry, birch and even spruce and hemlock.

Spotted Tussock Moth

The Spotted Tussock Moth caterpillar is brightly colored to show predators that it might be poisonous.

Food Plants: many different tree leaves such as mountain ash, apple, basswood, cherry, elm, maple and oak.

Milkweed Tussock Moth

Another caterpillar that uses bright colors to show that it might be poisonous. It is often found with its brothers and sisters on the same plant.

Food Plant: milkweed

Virginia Ctenucha

This fuzzy caterpillar is common in the fall. The beautiful adult can often be seen during the day in open fields.

Food Plants: mostly grasses but other plants as well.

Yellow Bear

The Yellow Bear is another fuzzy caterpillar, and it can be yellow, orange or brown. They sometimes even change color completely when they molt (see page 7).

Food Plants: many different kinds of trees and small plants.

Wooly Bear

The Wooly Bear is one of the best known of all caterpillars. It rolls into a ball when it is scared. It is very common in the fall, and it overwinters as a caterpillar.

Food Plants: grass, dandelions and nettles.

Books About Caterpillars

Caterpillars of Eastern North America
by David L. Wagner

This is a great book because it has so many caterpillars in it! There are 512 pages, and the pictures are nice and big.

Peterson First Field Guides: Caterpillars
by Amy Bartlett Wright

This book has drawings that show the differences between similar caterpillars. It is good for beginners.

Moths and Caterpillars of the North Woods
by Jim Sogaard

This book has really useful pictures and shows what both the moth and caterpillar look like.

The Girl Who Loved Caterpillars
by Jean Merrill

This is a story about a girl who wants to be different from everyone else and who likes caterpillars.

Index